Strike it Rich with

SILVER

in Coin Rolls

DAVID J. CONWAY

Published by

Krause Publications, a division of F+W Media, Inc.
700 East State Street • Iola, WI 54990-0001
715-445-2214 • 888-457-2873
www.krausebooks.com

To order books or other products call toll-free 1-800-258-0929
or visit us online at www.shopnumismaster.com

ISBN-13: 978-1-4402-3212-1
ISBN-10: 1-4402-3212-1

Cover Design by Jana Tappa
Designed by Sharon Bartsch
Edited by Debbie Bradley

Printed in U.S.A.

About the Author

 David Conway is a devoted coin collector and coin roll hunter. In 2007, he founded Cool-CashCoins, the coin appraisal business. In 2011, David created the *Gold and Silver Collections* iPhone application, making it easier to calculate the melt value of coins and jewelry.

David is from Wilton, Conn. He attends the George Washington University in Washington, DC, where he is majoring in business. David enjoys writing, jogging and traveling.

Acknowledgments

I would like to thank Debbie Bradley for seeing the potential in the original manuscript and for helping to create the amazing, finished book.

I would like to thank Jessica Joanlanne for the wonderful coin roll hunting illustrations.

I would also like to thank my Grandmother, Patricia Downing, for helping me to edit the original manuscript and grow my writing.

I would like to thank the incredible bank branches and tellers who make coin roll hunting possible.

Lastly, I would like to thank my amazing family, Mom, Dad, Scott, and Lelah, for supporting me and for always listening to me talk about this book.

Contents

CHAPTER ONE

Introduction

W hen Bob stopped by his local bank to make his usual deposit, he noticed a strange coin in the teller's tray.

"What's that?" he asked, eyeing the large coin.

"That," the teller responded, holding up the object, "is a half dollar coin. Would you like to buy it?"

Bob said "yes" and bought the coin. As it turns out, the teller had two more rolls of half dollars in the bank vault that she was eager to sell. She thought no other customer would want them, as there seemed to be little demand for them. Bob bought those rolls too – and immediately drove home to research his purchase.

Bob had traded $20.50 in change for 41 half dollar coins, also worth $20.50.

Surprisingly, Bob had received 41 silver half dollar coins from 1964. Although they looked exactly like any other ordinary Kennedy half dollar, these were special. At a market value of $35 per ounce of silver, these coins were actually worth $13 a piece. Bob's $20.50 roll of coins was actually about 15 ounces of pure silver worth over $500.

Is it really possible to find free silver? Absolutely. Today anyone can find silver in pocket change, or at

the bank, though years have passed since the last silver coin was minted for circulation.

The more you know about what to look for and the better you understand how to look the more silver you will find. In fact, an unlimited amount of silver and rare coins pass through our hands each day! Every week people give their coins to relatives, friends, children and grandchildren who, not pausing to check if the value of the coins has increased, dump hoards of precious silver at the bank or spend antique currency at the ice cream shop.

Can you hear the silver clinking as it flies out of the coin counter machine? Is your eye caught by the glimmer of light shining off of a strange looking piece in the bank teller's coin tray? It is our adventure, as coin roll hunters, to search for these coins and to appreciate a value in them that many others do not.

On the same day that society began using money, collectors began saving it. People always have saved money in its many forms and for many purposes. Humans have a natural tendency to save valuables for future use and for protection and security.

We save water, food, and money. As the concept of money developed, we even began using, and also saving, different types of currencies – namely coins and precious metals. The value of these currencies has become just as diverse as the forms of the currencies themselves.

People now collect and save coins and currency not just for later use, but also for collectible value. We collect coins for their monetary value, for security and stability, and for their scarcity, their intriguing designs, their history and importance in society, and even metallic value.

Over the past decade the demand for the intrinsic value of precious metals – gold and silver – within our coins has amplified. Today more than ever before, this commodity-based value within coins has surpassed the "collectible" value derived from condition, scarcity, and even historical importance of the pieces.

But this has not always been the case. In the past, the silver content of our coins did exceed the collectible or even the denominational "face value" of the currency. Our coins have been minted in gold and silver and our currency has been backed by precious metal guarantees.

Despite the rapid rises in metal prices, the average citizen remains unaware of the true significance of these older coins and consequently many silver pieces still circulate. The art of searching for these older coins and developing a deeper understanding and appreciation of their value is called coin roll hunting. Join the hunt.

What exactly is coin roll hunting? Simply described, coin roll hunting is the process of searching through rolls of coins in an attempt to find older or more valuable pieces. From simply checking occasional pocket change to ordering thousands of coins from banks, there are just as many ways to coin roll hunt as there are coins to search for. This book will provide you with both a general overview of coin roll hunting and an understanding of the various specific methods involved in this fascinating "hunt."

Silver is not biased. Regardless of your age, gender, personality or education, silver awaits your eager pockets. However, certain approaches will ensure that you find more silver than the average individual, and that you have a better overall experience searching for it.

Coin roll hunting is not complicated, but knowing what to expect is essential to success. With a small amount of information and a few hours of practice, you can be well on your way. It is important, however, to begin the hunt with a realistic approach. Just as a fisherman does not expect to reel in dozens of fish every single day, neither should the coin roll hunter expect to find silver coins on his first visit to the bank.

Could you strike it rich on the first day? Absolutely! Will this probably be the case? Nope. However, by hoping to find silver and not expecting to find silver, the coin roll hunter will embrace a realistic yet optimistic approach that will result not only in many great discoveries, but also in a more enjoyable experience. The thrill of the hunt does not lie in the "average" find, but in the rare and incredible find of gold and silver that is occasionally recovered, and in the excitement of anticipating this find

Q:

What is coin roll hunting?

A:

Coin roll hunting is the search for older, more valuable coins in circulation by looking through rolls of coins.

on each journey to the bank.

The methods of coin roll hunting are numerous. Some techniques can generate steady, almost guaranteed results, while others involve more risk but also more opportunity for greater rewards. Although some coin roll hunters prefer one practice over others, most pursue a combination of approaches. We suggest you try your hands at each method to see which you like most. The next chapter will describe in detail how coin roll hunting works and the steps you can take to get started.

Denomination	Coins Per Roll	Value of Roll	Rolls Per Box	Value of Box
Cent (Penny) $0.01	50	$0.50	50	$25
Nickel $0.05	40	$2.00	50	$100
Dime $0.10	50	$5.00	50	$250
Quarter $0.25	40	$10.00	50	$500
Half Dollar $0.50	20	$10.00	50	$500
Dollar $1.00	25 (maybe 20)	$25.00	50	$625

TERMINOLOGY |||||||||||||||||||||||||||||||||

CRH: Coin roll hunting

Keeper: Any coin worth saving

Skunked: Not finding any keepers

Box: Bank box of coin rolls

Roll: Bank roll of coins

Bag: Bank or coin counter bag of coins

Face value: Monetary worth of the denomination

BU: Brilliant uncirculated condition

90 percenter: 90 percent silver composition half dollar

40 percenter: 40 percent silver composition half dollar

Dump bank: Where searched coins are redeemed

Score: Finding one or more "keeper" coins

Clad: Copper, nickel or manganese alloy coins

Impaired proof: A coin taken from a proof set and spent

NIFC: Coins not intended for circulation

How
It Works

Steve Wilson had just finished his Saturday morning routine. The coffee had been made, the lawn mowed, the hedges trimmed, newspaper read, and still somehow it wasn't yet noon. With this delightful thought in mind, Steve started up his car, fastened his seat belt, and was off to the supermarket.

Jug of milk in hand, Steve approached the checkout line. The line was short, and he couldn't imagine an easier trip to the grocery. He pulled out his wallet and greeted the cashier.

"Good morning, how are you?"

She smiled. "Fine, thank you. And yourself?"

He smiled and reached for his credit card. Even the milk was on sale today.

He frowned. The card wasn't in his wallet. He checked his other pocket. Nothing. Where did he leave it last? He sighed. It was still on his night stand. He must have forgotten to put it away after ordering a book online the night before.

He shook his head and handed the cashier a $5 bill. Fortunately he had some cash left. Quickly, he paid the cashier and hurried back to the car, concerned about finding his credit card at home.

Back at home he was relieved to discover that the credit card was exactly where he had left it, on the night stand. He shook his head and tossed his wallet on the counter. There was a jingle.

Steve never carried coins around because he rarely paid with cash. The sound was strange to hear, and he knew it would become bothersome. He removed the coins from the wallet and tossed them onto the night stand. There was a shimmer of light. What was that coin?

A strange looking quarter lay atop the night stand. He picked it up, carried it over to the window for lighting, and examined the strange looking piece. On one side was a woman, on the other a large eagle. The coin looked very old and was quite worn. Could it be something valuable?

Steve eagerly searched the Internet for information, but could not find what he needed. Instead, he hurried off to the bookstore to purchase a coin guidebook. The quarter turned out to be a Standing Liberty quarter. It had been minted before the Washington quarter we use today. The attractive glimmer of light the coin produced and the strange chinking sound it made in his wallet took on a whole new meaning. The coin was silver, and even in the most worn down condition it was worth over $5. Steve purchased his jug of milk at the grocery store for free. That didn't happen every weekend.

Some more research revealed the many special

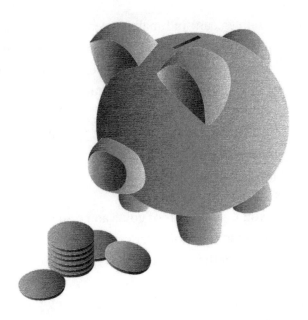

varieties of Standing Liberty quarters. Some of the dates, to his surprise, could be worth tens, hundreds, and even thousands of dollars. Steve laughed and hurried upstairs to the attic. Pocket change had taken on a whole new meaning, and so had that old change jar filled with coins. His search was just beginning.

Checking Your Change

Depending on the amount of time you are willing to dedicate, there are endless coin roll hunting possibilities. Most coin collectors are coin roll hunters on a casual basis – checking pocket change. Each day the average individual exchanges dozens of coins. Each year thousands more pass through our hands. The casual coin roll hunter can find many "keeper" coins worth saving by simply being aware of the change they use each day. Once you know what to keep an eye out for, checking your change becomes habitual and addicting.

The benefits of checking pocket change include:
• Takes little time and effort
• Becomes habitual
• Keeps you aware of your change
• Allows you to notice proof coins and rare dates
• Teaches you to look for error coins
• Allows you another way to search for silver coins

There really are no drawbacks to checking your pocket change. However, by only checking pocket change and not searching through rolls, you will examine a smaller volume of coins. For the average coin roll hunter, checking pocket change proves to be easy, fun, and not too time-consuming. And, by noticing and saving the occasional piece of currency, silver dime, or wheat back cent, one will easily amass a nice collection in several weeks.

The slower speed at which pocket change can be searched can be an advantage as well. Because of the smaller volume of coins to check, you can identify keepers more slowly and are therefore less likely to skip over rarities such as error or proof coins, which are easily overlooked when going through hundreds of bank wrapped rolls.

Ordering Boxes

Looking through the many rolls inside boxes of coins from banks is the other popular coin roll hunting approach. As shown in the previous chart, boxes can be ordered for any coin denomination. Note, however, that all boxes will contain exactly 50 rolls of coins. When buying a box from the bank, briefly check to ensure that it contains all 50 rolls. Most boxes will have punched holes on one side that you can quickly "eye ball" to see the ends of the coin rolls.

Boxes come in different shapes and sizes and will contain coin rolls with different types of wrappers from varying companies. Most, however, will be made of cardboard and will be heavy to carry. If you need to carry several boxes, be sure to park nearby. You might consider bringing a wheeled cart, duffel bag or small piece of luggage to transport your boxes of coins.

Although banks may have boxes of coins already in stock, they usually won't bring them out for you unless you request the teller to "check the vault" where most of the coin boxes are stored. For security purposes, banks will usually seal the vault prior to normal bank closing hours.

Additionally, at some banks, only the manager can open the vault. Expect to wait a couple of minutes if the manager must retrieve the box. To speed up the process, pay the teller your cash first (or fill out the withdrawal slip if you have an account) and then be patient as the teller hauls out the box.

If a bank does not have the assortment of boxes you are interested in, you may order boxes of coins from the bank.

The benefits of ordering boxes include:
• Guaranteed rolls of coins to search
• Large volume of coins to search
• Access to greater coin variety (such as half dollars)
• Easy to return searched coins if you have an account

Half dollar boxes are most commonly searched for silver. However, since they are out of style, banks may not carry halves in stock. In this case, you may order a box through the bank if you have an account there. If you do not have an account, the bank will not let you order. The teller will take your information or account number and in a few days your coins will be ordered. Some banks order coins weekly on a specific date, others bi-weekly. Confirm the expected coin arrival date with the teller so that you can receive your coins when they arrive.

As a courtesy, try to limit your orders to one or two boxes per week from each bank branch. Also, to keep the tellers happy, do not return your searched boxes of coins back to the same branch that you order coins from. Banks have been known to charge small fees for too many orders or to refuse orders altogether. (It may also be a good idea to bring in a small gift for your tellers as a kind gesture for their service. At the least, remember that please, thank you and a smile go a long way.)

A popular method of searching coin rolls from boxes involves simply peeling off the roll wrapper and spotting silver rims of coins. This approach is efficient, but only accurate after you have had some practice at recognizing the different colors of silver coins. As you go through each box of coins, try to check the face of each coin and not the rim, especially for your first few boxes. Although scanning the rims will allow you to easily re-tape the factory sealed rolls and quickly spot silver edges, it also will guarantee that you skip over not-intended-for-circulation, error and proof coins – all of which are valuable and exciting to find.

To return your searched box of coins you can either re-tape the factory roll wrappers, take your massive bag or pile of coins to a

Q:

What is the most efficient way to find silver coins?

A:

The best way to search for silver is to open rolls of dimes, quarters and half dollars and to look for silver rims.

coin counter machine, or re-wrap the coins into new rolls. Coin roll hunters use all three methods depending on whether they have extra coin rolls, their bank branch has a coin counter machine, and how good they are at re-taping old rolls.

I always have been a fan of re-wrapping the old rolls or re-rolling the coins into new rolls. Rolling the entire box usually does not take more than 10 minutes or so and allows the searcher to easily keep track of old rolls that they already have searched. Simply draw an X or a dash with a sharpie on each roll, and you will recognize the rolls if they cross your path again.

Note: Be sure to replace any removed coins with regular ones so that the rolls are not short of coins!

Visiting Banks and Road Trips

Many coin roll hunters will simply visit banks and ask for rolls of coins that they can then buy and search through in the car or at home. Visiting banks is an effective way of finding new coins to search. Because half dollars are more difficult to find in circulation, coin roll hunters will travel from bank to bank asking for rolls of half dollar coins. Although many banks will not have any (or will have only a few dollars worth), some may have a dozen rolls or so and possibly a full box.

It is good to know that going to banks to ask for

half dollar coins is largely hit or miss. Most of the coin rolls of half dollars at banks either contain large quantities of silver dropped off by the unsuspecting inheritor, or rolls of coins already searched and dumped by another coin roll hunter. Sometimes these coin rolls will have already been marked – but sometimes they will not be. Occasionally luck may grant you full rolls of older coins including Walking Liberty and Franklin halves. These are real finds!

The benefits of traveling to banks include:
• Spend more time searching
• More variety in location
• Potential for larger scores of silver
• Explore unsearched coin areas

Traveling to banks is the riskiest and most time-consuming option for coin roll hunters, but despite the difficulties, "road trips" are extremely exciting and offer opportunity for great reward if a hoard

Q:

How many silver coins are usually in each roll?

A:

Usually, zero. However, you will frequently find one or two silver coins and occasionally even an entire roll of all silver coins. These are worth tens to hundreds of dollars.

of older coins has been deposited at the bank. Don't be afraid to visit nearby banks while on vacation. The largest silver scores do not remain at banks for very long, but if the tellers or other customers have not identified the silver yet, you may discover a massive silver half dollar cache.

Checking Change:
- Receive coins as change from stores
- Briefly scan coins for older pieces and varieties
- Spend or pocket remainder of coins as usual

Ordering Boxes:
- Open a checking account at bank branch and order a box of coins
- Search through coins (or just check rims for silver)
- Reroll coins or take to a coin machine to return

Visiting Banks:
- Travel to local or distant bank branches
- Ask for older coins, currency, or rolls of half dollars
- Save rolls, search, and return to your dump bank

CHAPTER THREE

Why to search and what to find

Mary had been home from college for the summer for two weeks. After sleeping around the clock and hanging out with the family for a week straight, reality set in. She needed to keep herself busy, and making some money would certainly help pay for next year's trip at spring break. Her friends were hoping to visit the Bahamas, and nothing would stop her from going with them. Well, nothing except for money.

Mary hung up a few flyers and quickly found a few babysitting jobs. She had a fun time playing with the kids, but when August rolled around she began to worry about having enough cash for the school year.

On her last babysitting job for the summer she took two little girls miniature golfing. Afterward, to quell a wave of afternoon tiredness, she took the kids to the local ice cream shop. As they left the store she noticed that the shopping center had installed a new coin counting machine. As they passed it on the way to the car, something caught her eye. There were coins in the tray. She quickly tossed out her ice cream cone and scooped up the dimes someone had left behind.

Mary forgot about the coins until a week later. It

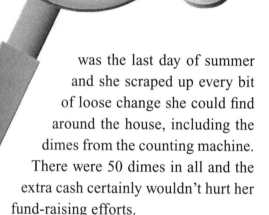

was the last day of summer and she scraped up every bit of loose change she could find around the house, including the dimes from the counting machine. There were 50 dimes in all and the extra cash certainly wouldn't hurt her fund-raising efforts.

Exhausted from all the hard work babysitting, she flopped onto the couch to watch some T.V. Commercials were always annoying, but today one of them actually sounded important.

"We buy old coins, gold, silver," shouted the announcer. "We pay top dollar!"

Her dimes were on the screen.

Mary ran to her father's desk and grabbed the old coin book he had saved from when he was a kid. She scanned the pages, eagerly looking for her coins.

"Anything minted before 1965 will be silver," the book said about dimes.

But weren't these just ordinary old Roosevelt dimes? Why were they so special? She then found a chart describing the silver content of the coins, and the value for each price of silver.

Mary sifted through the coins until she found one that looked different than the others. What was the strange looking dime from 1916? She double-checked the book and realized that she was holding a Mercury dime. It was nearly 100 years old!

Mary was fascinated. Her numismatic knowledge was already improving. She turned the dime around slowly in her hand, holding it carefully by the rim so as not to damage the face of the coin. She then checked the mintmark. The letter was small and worn, but just legible enough to see. It was a "D." This coin had been produced in the Denver mint!

At face value, Mary's change is worth just a couple of dollars. But when silver prices hover around $30 a troy ounce, Mary's dimes are worth over $100.

What about the 1916-D Mercury dime that she found? That coin is worth over $1,000. Mary was definitely going on that spring break trip. Good thing she checked the coin book for unbiased values.

The reasons for coin roll hunting are just as diversified as its methods. Coin collectors may scan pocket change hoping to find every date of penny from 1909

A silver Peace dollar

through 2012. A bullion lover may purchase boxes of half dollars weekly hoping to acquire a hoard of silver to sell or save for retirement. Another coin collector may visit banks while on vacation so that she can discover scarce error coins, antique currency, impaired proofs, or even uncirculated rolls of modern coinage. Although your reasons for searching through coins may influence your coin roll hunting strategy, whatever your goals or methods, the treasures sought are the same. Those treasures are many.

The most obvious reason people search through coins is to find older or interesting pieces for a collection. Coin roll hunting may help you achieve a collecting goal such as "assemble a complete collection of cents from 1909 through 2011" or "find all of the presidential dollars and state quarters in uncirculated rolls" or, you may simply wish to save anything unique or scarce, such as error coins or classic designs (Buffalo nickels, Wheat cents, Mercury dimes).

The possibilities for collecting coins are endless. Rare and expensive varieties of coins are found daily – including scarce date impaired proof coins.

To fully appreciate the hobby of coin collecting make sure you understand the specific characteristics that determine the value of a coin. The most important are: scarcity/mintage figures, date/mintmark, condition, metal content, variety or design, denomination, and current market demand. Accurately determining the condition of a coin is difficult and takes some time to learn. Because precious metal prices fluctuate daily and are essential to evaluating silver and gold coins, try to keep up-to-date with the current coin market.

Error coins are coins that were struck differently (in error) by the mint and are the result of mistakes made during the minting process. An error coin is a coin that was not minted the way it should have

Q:

What is the most profitable coin roll hunting find to look for?

A:

Search for silver dimes and quarters minted 1964 and earlier and for silver half dollar coins minted 1970 and earlier to get the most profit.

been. Pennies struck in nickel metal or dimes with two dates printed over each other are examples of error coins.

The common types of error coins include clipped planchets, lamination errors, and die errors such as die cracks, over-dates, reprinted dates, broad-strike, and wrong planchets.

Clipped planchet coins will be irregularly shaped or missing a small piece of the coin.

Lamination errors occur when metal within the coin has separated.

Die cracks will result in extra, unnecessary cracks deep into the coins surface.

Over-dates and reprinted dates produce coins with extra dates, mintmarks, or even entire obverses or reverses.

Broad-strike coins are coins that were struck entirely off-center, meaning that although the coin has its proper shape, the image itself was printed inappropriately onto the coins surface.

Collectors commonly collect "blank planchet" coins. These are just metal with no image printed on the face of the coins at all.

Lastly, any coin manufactured with the wrong metal (a dime struck of copper) is a wrong planchet coin.

Error coins represent a large portion of the coin-collecting marketplace and come in many, often times unusual, varieties – cents struck in nickel, currency minted off center, large die plates, and many more. I recommend and urge you to buy a book to learn more about the particular varieties and how to distinguish them from other coins.

All coin roll hunters search for silver coins. Silver coins are older, generally minted in scarcer designs, and, because of their precious metal content, are always worth more than face value. These characteristics place silver coins at the heart of the CRH hobby. Every type of coin roll hunter inevitably hopes to find and save silver coins from circulation.

However, CRHs chose to search primarily or only for silver coins. Silver coins are older coins that were minted in silver composition when our coinage was backed by precious metal content and our currency's value was based on the gold standard. Traditionally dimes, quarters, half dollars, and dollar coins were minted in 90 percent silver composition.

After 1964, the Mint replaced all silver coins, except for those minted in silver proof sets or special commemorative pieces, with copper, nickel and clad coins (coins made of copper, nickel, and zinc). Some exceptions include half dollar coins, which were then minted in 40 percent silver composition from 1965-1970, and silver war nickels, which were struck in 35 percent silver content for World War II efforts from 1942-1945.

Although the process of producing silver coins for general circulation was replaced by clad production nearly half a century ago, many silver coins still cir-

Monticello, mint mark above reverse

1943/2P

Silver war nickel

culate today. Throughout the 1960s, many collectors pulled aside every silver piece they could find and, as the decades progressed, the ratio of silver to clad coins circulating steadily declined. The soaring commodity prices and the Great Recession resulted in an even greater number of silver coins being pulled from circulation.

But, just as the hard times have led to more silver searchers, the recession also has led to more people breaking out their old coin collections and cashing them in at the bank. Due to the high prices of gold and silver, the volume of silver coins entering and exiting general circulation again has increased significantly. Moreover, on a profit basis, the rising value of silver has more than compensated for any slight decrease in the proportion of silver coins circulating.

Furthermore, silver searchers need not worry about there being a shortage of silver in circulation. In fact, the higher the silver prices, the greater the volume of silver entering and exiting our change. As coin collectors and searchers find silver coins, they save them. Eventually they either sell those coins to a coin store that melts them down or resells the coins to another collector, or they save the coins and pass them on to children, grandchildren, and inheritors.

The people who receive these coins are not collectors, and consequently, they frequently spend the coins at stores or deposit them in rolls to their local bank. These processes ensure a continuous cycle of silver entering and exiting circulation.

Despite the patterns tracing the quantity and price of silver, the searcher always will receive greater value when finding coins instead of buying them. When silver prices are high more people search for silver, so there will be less to find, but the value of the coins found will be proportionately greater. Although the probability of finding a silver coin will decrease, the value of finding it will increase.

When silver prices are lower, fewer people search for coins in

Q:

How much silver is still in circulation?

A:

There is an unlimited amount of silver to be found in change and at the bank. People will always continue to accidentally spend valuable silver coins.

circulation, but more people, because of the lower value of silver, will spend the coins and introduce them back into circulation. When silver prices are lower there is less incentive for collectors to retrieve full silver melt value for their coins – and there also is less incentive for coin roll hunters to save coins. As a result, there will be more silver coins in circulation to find, albeit at lower values.

A coin's value, to varying degrees, is composed of different parts, and consequently each affects price differently as it changes. As commodity prices fluctuate relative to other prices (such as inflation, cost of living, etc.), they also influence the relative collectible value of the coin itself.

A silver Mercury dime from 1928, for example, will currently fetch its silver melt value of $2.50 in average circulated condition. A similar coin, a 1964 Roosevelt dime, also struck in silver, will sell for the same $2.50. But, if the value of silver was to drop from $35 an ounce to $15 an ounce, the coins' values will not drop proportionately.

The older Mercury dime will retain more of its "collector value" because of its unique age, scarcity, and design than will the recent 1964 Roosevelt dime. The 1964 dime would still sell for its silver value (in

this case about $1.25), but the Mercury dime might still be valued at $2 or more.

There are several defining characteristics of silver coinage that help distinguish them from clad coinage in circulation. Although not all silver coins you encounter will have older designs (some of our current Roosevelt dimes were made in silver once and will appear no differently to the untrained eye), in reality coins minted prior to 1965 are unique because they contain silver. These silver coins have a slightly different coloring, they tone (change color) differently

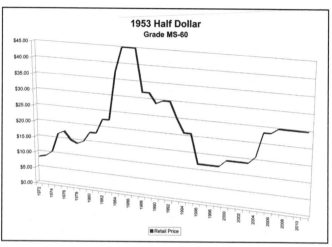

Retail price of 1953 half dollar over time

over time, and they even make a distinctive clinking sound when dropped.

The different coloration of the rims on silver coins makes checking the rims of money the most effective technique for identifying silver. Light reflects off of the edge of silver pieces making them easily identifiable. It's best to gather some silver coins and study how the rims look compared to clad coins.

Check the actual faces of coins first so that you know for certain what you are looking at is a silver composition coin. Then you can practice looking for silver by the rim without missing any coins. Despite the high level of accuracy associated with experience, even the professional can only hope to achieve near-perfection.

Know your dates. Roosevelt dimes made of silver were produced prior to 1965.

To find proof coins and other valuable varieties, it is important to check the face of each coin. The rim of a proof coin will typically appear the same as the rim of any other coin in circulation. However, the face of a proof coin, even a well-circulated one, will have a reflective surface. Overall though, rim-checking proves to be the most efficient way to find silver coins because it allows the searcher to easily seal back open coin rolls without having to separate the coins into a pile. Silver rims are identifiable by

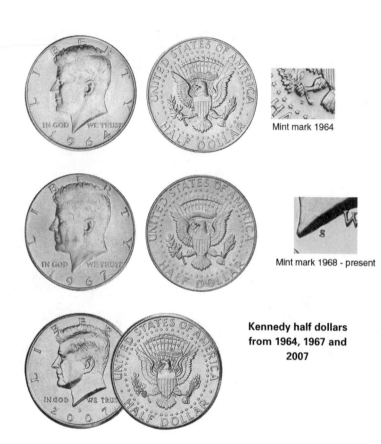

Mint mark 1964

Mint mark 1968 - present

Kennedy half dollars from 1964, 1967 and 2007

Silver Coin Chart:

Denomination	Years	Composition	Silver Weight	Appearance
Nickel	1942-1945	35%	0.05626 oz	Jefferson
Dime	Pre-1965	90%	0.07234 oz	Roosevelt & pre
Quarter	Pre-1965	90%	0.18084 oz	Washington & pre
Early Half Dollar	Pre-1965	90%	0.36169 oz	Kennedy & pre
Later Half Dollar	1965-1970	40%	0.14790 oz	Kennedy

MAIN COIN VARIETIES YOU WILL ENCOUNTER

Cent: Indian Head (1859-1909),
Wheat (1909-1958), Lincoln (1959-Present)

Nickel: Buffalo (1913-1938),
Jefferson (1939-Present)

Dime: Mercury (1916-1942),
Roosevelt (1946-Present)

Quarter: Washington (1932-Present)

Half Dollar: Walking Liberty (1916-1947),
Franklin (1948-1963), Kennedy
(1964-Present NIFC)

Dollar: Eisenhower (IKE) (1971-1978),
Susan B. Anthony (1979-1999), Sacagawea
(2000-2009), Presidential (2009-Present)

their distinguished silver color.

• Although many other coin varieties contain silver, they are too rare to encounter in circulation. Coin collectors see them often, though.

• 1964 first-year Kennedy half dollars were struck in 90 percent silver.

What to look for

Phil used to collect coins when he was a kid. Although he really knew very little about the coins, he still saved his old coin books, just in case. When his two kids, Jane and Garrett, got into coin collecting in middle school, he was relieved to find the coin books in the basement, still intact and hardly worn.

Purchasing a $25 box of pennies from the bank became a weekly tradition for Phil, Jane and Garrett. Every Sunday evening the family would go through the box of pennies, tear open the rolls, and search through the coins. With three people working together the box only took a few minutes to search. Soon they started purchasing several boxes.

For Thanksgiving break the family decided to get mom involved too. They bought $100 in pennies (that's 200 rolls!) for the long weekend. After turkey and mashed potatoes, all were eager to begin the search.

"I found one!" Shouted Jane. "Me too!" yelled Garrett. Cries of excitement rang out all evening while they say by the fire, fervently searching for keepers. Together they found nearly 100 wheat cents. Three of them were even steel cents made in 1943 for the war effort.

Garrett was assigned the task of checking the dates of the wheat cents. Although they hadn't found anything too rare yet, he was always on the lookout for that elusive 1909-S VDB cent, which could be worth thousands.

"Find anything?" asked Jane, yawning and ready for bed. There was a pause.

"I think so," said Garrett hesitantly. "Let me go get the magnifying glass, I can't quite read the date. I think it's a 1909."

A few minutes later he ran back into the living room, feet pounding the floor. He cried out, "We finally found one!" The family hurried over to examine the coin.

The wheat penny they discovered did not have the famous VDB signature on the reverse. However, it did have the special "S" mintmark. Garrett had unearthed a very special 1909-S Lincoln wheat cent. This penny was produced the first year the wheat cent design was released. The "S" mintmark revealed that the coin was minted in San Francisco.

The penny was worth nearly $200! They decided to save the coin rather than sell it. Their collection was growing. They would definitely be picking up some more pennies at the bank next weekend. All they needed now was a VDB and a few more semi-key dates and they would have the complete collection.

All that glitters is not silver

Although hunting rolls of coins to snatch the elusive silver coin that will reap rewards due to its weight in silver, there are other coins to be on the lookout for.

So in addition to checking the rims of dimes, quarters, and half dollar coins in search of a lighter, whiter, silver rim that best identifies silver coins, keep you eyes open for other coins of value.

Proof Coins

Proof coins are coins that were minted specially by the United States Mint and included in proof sets. These coins have mirror-like frosty or reflective surfaces.

Proof coins are produced using polished dies. The coins are then double-struck to enhance the detail of the design. Most proof coins will also have an "S" mintmark, which indicates that they were struck at the San Francisco Mint. Although almost all proof coins are struck in San Francisco today, a few varieties, including the silver Eagle bullion proof coins, are struck at the West Point Mint and feature a "W" mintmark. Proof coins released before 1968 were instead made at the Philadelphia Mint.

If you are only checking the rims of coins, you will probably not find any proof pieces, as they are best identified by their surface. Some proof coins can be very valuable, others not as much. Proof coins that have been broken out of their original sets are called impaired proofs. In circulation they may still be in proof or proof-like condition. Depending on the date, scratched proof coins will not retain much value.

1998 Kennedy half dollar proof

Cents

The Lincoln cent was introduced in 1909 to commemorate the centennial year of Abraham Lincoln's birth.

It was the first time the United States included a portrait on a regular issue coin intended for circulation.

This coin features a portrait of our 16th President on the obverse and wheat ears on the reverse; it was minted from 1909 through 1958. Though most wheat cents were produced in vast quantities, there are a few rarities to look out for.

For example, the 1909 wheat cent with an "S" San Francisco mintmark can be worth hundreds of dollars. A 1909-S wheat cent with the initials "VDB" on the bottom reverse of the coin can be worth over a $1,000 and is a favorite among coin collectors.

The VDB initials belong to the coin's designer, Victor David Brenner, and were included on the reverse of only a few 1909 coins. Other rare "key date" wheat cents include the 1911-S, 1914-D, 1922 (no mintmark), and the 1931-S. Wheat pennies are fun to collect because of the many different key and semi-key dates needed to complete the full set.

Although the Lincoln cent obverse did not change with the 1959 redesign, the wheat ears reverse was replaced with the Lincoln Memorial.

The Lincoln Memorial cent, with Lincoln on the

obverse and the Memorial on the reverse, has been minted since 1959 when it was introduced to replace the wheat back penny. The wheat cent has Lincoln on the obverse and a pair of wheat ears and the writing "ONE CENT" on the reverse. The wheat cent was minted from 1909 through 1958. Before the wheat penny, the Indian Head cent (1859-1909), the Flying Eagle cent (1856-1858) and a variety of large cent coins about the size of half dollars were used.

The reverse design changed again in 2009 to honor the bicentennial anniversary of Lincoln's birth. Four reverse designs were produced in 2009 to reflect four different stages of Lincoln's life and career. In 2010, the reverse design was changed to a Union shield.

1909 Lincoln wheat cent

Things to Save

- Wheat cents or coins minted prior to 1959
- Proof coins
- Any error variety or special date / condition coin

How to Search

Search cents by buying rolls or boxes or checking change

- Open the roll of pennies and pour them out
- Scan the coins in your hand and remove any keepers
- Check reverse of coin for design other than Memorial and obverse of coin for dates of 1958 and earlier
- Replace removed coins with regular ones and re-roll

The Lincoln Memorial cent was made of 95 percent copper until 1982, when the composition was changed from copper to mainly zinc to avoid high production costs resulting from rising copper prices.

According to U.S. law, the cent design cannot be changed more often than every 25 years. The 50-year change has been coincidental.

Nickels

The Buffalo nickel, also called the Indian head nickel, was minted from 1913 through 1938. The obverse of this coin features a portrait of a Native American and the reverse depicts a grazing bison.

The Buffalo nickel was produced in San Francisco, Denver and Philadelphia. The "S" and "D" mintmarks can be found on the bottom reverse of the coin – but remember, coins minted in Philadelphia do not have a mintmark.

Buffalo nickels were designed with such great raised detail that they are easily worn flat in circulation. Consequently, many "dateless" Buffalo nickels survive and make specific dates very rare.

The 1913 "3-1/2 or 3 legged" Buffalo nickel is worth hundreds of dollars, even in worn condition. As the name describes, this special 1913 variety was produced with a bison missing one leg. Also keep an eye out for any scarce "D" or "S" mintmark coins dated

1927 or earlier.

The Mint introduced the Jefferson nickel in 1938 with a portrait of Jefferson on the obverse and the image of his home, Monticello, on the reverse.

Buffalo nickel minted 1914-1938

Jefferson nickels have traditionally been minted in nickel. However, from 1942-1945 nickels were struck in 35 percent silver to assist the World War II war effort. Although these coins have a slightly differ-ent coloration, unlike other silver coins the rim alone cannot identify them. Silver war nickels can be classi-fied by their dates (1942-1945) and by the position of the mintmark, which was moved to the reverse above the image of Monticello throughout the production years.

To honor the Lewis and Clark expedition bicenten-nial and Louisiana Pur-

- BU Jefferson nickels from 1959 and earlier
- Silver war nickels from 1942-1945
- Earlier date Jefferson pieces 1959 and earlier
- Proof coins

How to Search

Search nickels by buying rolls or boxes or checking change

- Open the roll of nickels and poor them out
- Scan the coins in your hand and remove any keepers
- Check dates on coins
- Replace removed coins with regular ones and re-roll

chase, the Jefferson nickel reverse was redesigned for 2004 and 2005. There were two unique designs produced for each year. The first reverse design for 2004 features Indian Peace Medals. The second reverse design for 2004 is an image of the keelboat used for the Lewis and Clark expedition.

In 2005, the reverse design again changed to depict an American bison. The second design for the year shows a beautiful coastline view. The phrase "Ocean in view! O! The joy!" was also included beside the coastline. These words come from a journal entry that William Clark made when exploring the west.

In 2005, the obverse image of Jefferson was also changed to show a bust of Jefferson looking to the right. Joe Fitzgerald designed the new bust of Jefferson for that year.

Beginning in 2006, the reverse again depicted Monticello. However, the new image of Monticello was sharpened to more clearly portray the monument. The obverse of the coin was replaced with a forward facing portrait of Jefferson. Both of these designs are still produced today, and are more detailed than the older, pre-2004 Jefferson and Monticello designs.

Dimes

The Mercury dime was designed by Adolph A. Weinmenn to replace the previously produced Barber dime. It was produced from 1916 through 1945, except for the years 1922, 1932, and 1933. The Mercury dime actually portrays the winged head of Liberty on the obverse. However, the image more closely resembles the Roman god Mercury, which led to the name "Mercury dime."

Although the 90 percent silver Mercury dime weighs 2.5 grams and contains .07234 ounces of precious metal, many scarcer varieties should certainly not be redeemed for melt value. The 1916-D, 1921, and 1921-D are each worth hundreds to thousands of dollars, depending on condition. In 1942, at the start of World War II, some dimes were accidentally re-struck, creating the elusive 1942 "2 over 1" and 1942-D "2 over 1" varieties. It is definitely worth double-checking for these rarities!

The Roosevelt dime has been produced since 1946, when it was first designed to honor the deceased President Franklin D. Roosevelt. Although our modern Roosevelt dimes are made of copper-nickel-clad, dimes dated 1964 and earlier were struck in 90 percent silver composition, and contain .07234 ounces of the precious metal. The reverse of this coin bears a torch wrapped in oak and olive branches. Check for silver rims to best identify the silver, pre-1965 Roosevelt dimes.

From 1946 to present the classic Roosevelt dime has been in use. Although the design of the coin has not changed, the government altered the composition from 90 percent silver to copper nickel clad after the year 1964. Prior to the Roosevelt dime, there was the Mercury dime, the Barber dime, the Seated dime, and Bust dimes. You will mainly encounter silver Roosevelt dimes or the occasional Mercury dime when hunting through coin rolls.

Mint mark 1946-64

The Roosevelt dime was introduced in 1946.

Things to Save

- Any silver Roosevelt dime or other dime dated 1964 and earlier
- Proof coins

How to Search

- Search dimes by buying rolls or boxes or checking change
- Open the roll of dimes and poor the coins carefully into your hand in a row
- Scan the rims of the coins and remove any silver keepers
- Poor coins back into roll and reseal or re-tape edge of roll

Quarters

Prior to the Washington quarter, Standing Liberty quarters, Barber quarters, Seated Liberty quarters, and Bust quarters of various designs (all produced in silver) were issued. Washington quarters received a special 1776-1976 Bicentennial reverse design in 1976 but these coins are of little value unless they are of the special silver variety produced in some mint sets.

The Washington quarter was produced with the eagle reverse from 1932 through 1998. This coin was designed by John Flanagan, weighs 6.25 grams, and, like silver dimes and half dollars, was also produced in 90 percent silver composition prior to 1965.

A silver Washington quarter contains .18084 ounces of pure silver. Though many of the silver variety were hoarded in the late 1960s after the metal content was changed to copper-nickel-clad, many older pieces can still be found in circulation. Washington quarters from 1964 and earlier appear the same as non-silver varieties, but reflect the distinctive silver colored rim and are frequently found in circulation today. The 1932 "D" and "S" quarters are the scarcest, and most valuable key dates in the Washington coin collection.

In 1999, the United States introduced the popular state quarter program. This popular program, featuring reverse designs that honor each state and territory, led to a surge of individuals checking pocket change for state quarters and eventually to an onslaught of new coin collectors and investors.

This boom contributed greatly to the past decade's increases in coin prices and coin collecting popularity. Although more collectors indicate greater demand and higher prices, their activity also creates greater market volume and therefore more stable and accurate pricing and more liquidity (ability to buy and sell a coin) to others. The Internet and eBay also have contributed to this market growth.

At the completion of the state quarter program, Congress authorized the launch of the America the Beautiful

Mint mark 1932-64

Washington quarter was introduced in 1932.

Things to Save

- Any silver Washington quarter or other quarter dated 1964 and earlier
- Proof coins
- Any statehood quarter that you may need in your collection

How to Search

- Search quarters by buying rolls or boxes or checking change
- Open the roll of quarters and pour the coins into your hand in a row
- Scan the rims of the coins and remove any silver keepers
- Place coins back into roll and reseal or re-tape edge of roll

state quarter program featuring parks and landmarks from each state and territory. That program launched in 2010.

The state and national parks quarters have the same portrait of Washington on the obverse.

Half Dollars

The Walking Liberty half dollar was produced from 1916 through 1947. Adolph A. Weinman designed this coin the same year he designed the Mercury dime.

This half dollar weighs 12.5 grams and was struck in 90 percent silver composition (.36169 ounces of pure silver) throughout the entire mintage period. Walking Liberty half dollars from 1919-D, 1921, 1921-D, 1921-S, and 1938 D are very rare. Additionally, 1917-S half dollars with the "S" mintmark printed on the obverse are scarce and very valuable. Walking Liberty half dollars are sometimes called "Walkers" for short.

The Franklin half dollar replaced the Walking Liberty half in 1948 and was produced through 1963. Though these coins were minted in large quantities, pieces in superb condition can be much more valuable. Mint state (MS) condition Franklin half dollars may even have full bell lines on the coin reverse. If the lines running across the bottom of the Liberty bell are fully percepti ble, the full bell lines coin is of especially good condition.

Mint mark

1950 Franklin half dollar

All Franklins were minted in 90 percent sil- ver composition, and also contain .36169 ounces of silver. The lucky coin roll hunter has been known to stumble on a full roll of Franklin half dollars.

The Kennedy half dollar was designed by Gilroy Roberts and Frank Gasparro and was introduced in 1964. Although we still produce the Kennedy half dollar today, the Mint ceased releasing the coin for general circulation in 2001. Since then, half dollar coins have been minted in proof sets and in special uncirculated rolls that can only be ordered from the mint.

These coins are common but do carry premium value if found in uncirculated condition. Occasionally whole rolls of these coins are found. Save these and keep them unopened.

Besides the special 1776-1976 Bicentennial reverse design used in 1976, the Kennedy half dollar design has not changed since it was introduced in 1964. Kennedy half dollars were produced in 90 percent silver composition in 1964 and later in 40 percent silver from 1965-1970 before being replaced by the all clad variety in 1971. Preceding the Kennedy halves were the Franklin, Walking Liberty, Barber, Seated, and Bust halves (all silver).

The 1776-1976 Bicentennial half dollars are not rare. In fact, they are commonly circulated today. However, in some mint sets 1976 half dollars were coined in 40 percent silver content. Coin roll hunters can spot these coins by checking the rim. Remember, keep an eye out for older, silver commemorative half dollars too! These can be worth hundreds to thousands of dollars.

Dollars

Originally, dollar coins were large, heavy coins made of silver. The Mint produced Bust dollars, Seated dollars, Trade dollars, Morgan dollars (the classic silver dollar of the West), and Peace dollars.

The last silver dollar in circulation was the 1935 Peace dollar coin. Following the Peace dollar, we did not produce any more dollar coins until 1971 when, for several years, Ike or Eisenhower dollars were coined. Although this coin was made of clad, many 40 percent silver proof and "not issued for circulation" examples were made.

Subsequently, another dollar coin was not produced until 1979, when the first small-sized dollar coin (about the width of a quarter) was made: the Susan B. Anthony dollar. This coin was eventually replaced by the Sacagawea gold small dollar coin in 2000. Most recently the small (and still gold colored) Presidential dollar coin was introduced in 2007.

1973
Eisenhower
dollar

Despite numerous efforts by the United States mint endorsing these dollar coins,

$1 coins

Things to Save

- Any large-sized dollar coins
- Proof coins
- Uncirculated rolls

How to Search

- Search dollars by asking banks for large-sized ones or un-open rolls
- Keep unopened rolls sealed unless they are hand wrapped
- Search hand-wrapped rolls or bags of large-sized dollars
- Save all large-sized pieces and BU small-sized dollar rolls

the public has not accepted them as replacements for the dollar bill.

In 2012, striking Presidential dollars for circulation was suspended and going forward, only enough coins will be struck to meet the demand for collectors. However, they are very exciting pieces to save and collect, especially when sealed in uncirculated rolls.

Gold and Silver Bullion

Although extremely uncommon, occasionally a rare gold piece does enter circulation. Sometimes collectors mistakenly spend modern bullion coins, or even vintage gold pieces from the early 19th and 20th centuries.

In the 2000s I found a one-quarter ounce gold bullion coin ($5 face value) in a roll of quarters. This coin is worth over $400. Silver Eagles (modern silver bullion coins) are taken to the bank more frequently than one would expect. Keep an eye out for these incredible finds.

American Eagle silver dollar

CHAPTER FIVE

Banks and etiquette

How to exchange searched coins

Linda walked the block twice during her lunch break each day. The past few days had been rainy, though, and the feeling of being trapped indoors weighed heavily upon her. Today it was forecasted to rain. There was even a 30 percent chance of thundershowers. Linda didn't know how she was going to make it.

Then, just before lunch break, the sun peaked through the clouds. Linda broke out her sneakers and slipped outside just as the wet pavement began to dry.

She had been coin roll hunting casually for nearly a year, and missed her daily walk for another reason besides the weather entirely. On the block she would walk by her local bank and ask if they had any half dollar coins. She had called the bank earlier. Today was her lucky day.

Inside the bank branch she waited in line anxiously and then greeted the teller, a woman she had never met before. The teller must have transferred from another branch.

"Hello. I called earlier. I am here to pick up a few rolls of old half dollar coins. Do you have them?" asked Linda.

The teller frowned. "Sorry, they are in the vault."

Linda sighed. "Could you please get them? I really want to buy them and would appreciate it."

The teller smirked. "I am sorry, they are silver and I am planning on buying them later."

Linda was furious. "What? I am a customer. Can't I buy them? I called!"

"Do you have an account with us?" the teller asked angrily.

Linda sighed. She was furious, but knew that the bank would never let her take the coins when the teller wanted them if she didn't have an account.

Bummed, she left the bank and returned to work. Next week she would open a checking account. Next week she would be prepared.

Wait a minute. She didn't get to keep the coins? No silver hoard? Can't we at least know what was in those rolls? What a horrible story!

We take a brief break from the happy-go-lucky coin roll hunting narrative to reveal how any searching scenario can go awry. Not every bank has silver coins for you. The rolls Linda wanted to purchase may have contained lots of silver, or they may have contained nothing of value. We will never know for sure, and neither will Linda. Adhere to the following guidelines to ensure that your coin roll hunting experience is a positive one. But don't worry, unlike the other more encouraging anecdotes so far, Linda's was made up. But it does happen – often.

Although most bank tellers are extremely helpful, some may not be as competent or pleasant as others. If your teller is having a bad day, always be kind and he or she will return the favor.

CRHs face two types of challenges when visiting banks or ordering coin rolls and boxes: personal obstacles and procedural or "company" obstacles.

Personal challenges are challenges related to the way you as the customer and the bank tellers or managers interact. Typically tellers and clients are polite and the bank visit occurs smoothly, but sometimes awkward or uncomfortable situations are unavoidable. For example, bank tellers are there to help you (it's their job) and they are happy to do so, but if the teller has told you several times that there are no coins in the vault, trust him, and don't force him to go and check. Enjoying your morning and not getting any coins is better than fighting to find a few half

Saint-Gaudens $20 gold coin

dollars that will probably end up being clad. Be kind to bank tellers and they will be kind to you. Establish lasting relationships with the bank employees. Next time you visit they may have put aside some special silver coins just for you.

Important: Always remember to replace the coins you remove from rolls with regular coins before you return them back to the bank or make an exchange. No one wants to receive a short roll of coins.

Common Personal Challenges and Solutions

Challenge: The bank teller says she has no half dollar coins.

Solution: Politely ask her if the other tellers have any or if the bank may have some in the vault.

Challenge: The tellers do not have the coins you need, and they tell you that the vault does not have any.

Solution: They are either correct and the vault doesn't have the coin rolls you need – OR they are too busy to check, and asking again won't get them to do so. In both cases move on and don't waste any more time there.

Procedural or company challenges are obstacles formed by the regulations of the bank, the law, security standards, and corporate policy. Although disagreements relating to these principles frustrate the banking customer, they are usually there for the protection of both you and the bank. Fortunately, they are not very difficult to work around if you follow the appropriate solutions.

Common Procedural Challenges and Solutions

Challenge: Bank teller will not take your rolled coins, let you use the coin counter, or sell you any of the bank's coins.

Solution: Always remember, they are not required to! Most banks will sell you coins in exchange for cash but to swap coins for coins or to order boxes you usually need an account. Checking accounts are not difficult to open.

Challenge: You have an account but the bank won't order you the boxes of coins that you need.

Solution: Almost all banks only order coins weekly or bi-weekly. Do not order more than one or two boxes of coins from each bank branch per week.

Challenge: You have an account but the bank wants to charge you a fee for ordering boxes.

Solution: Either pay the small fee or, better yet, order your coins from another branch. Limiting your orders to one box each week will prevent banks from instituting fees.

How to Order Boxes of Coins

- Set up an account at the bank
- Have enough money in the account
- Do not order more than one or two boxes each week
- Always thank the tellers and bring them a small gift every so often
- Establish positive relationships with tellers and they will facilitate your visit

Standard procedures for exchanging coins:
- Make sure your rolls are not short if coins were removed
- Mark your rolls with a line in sharpie so you know they were searched
- You will usually need an account to exchange rolls of coins or use a coin counting machine

Standard procedures for visiting any bank:
- Be polite to the tellers and managers
- Opening a free checking or savings account will make things easier
- Do not pursue arguments with employees or other customers

Check the requirements for opening an account at your local bank. Typically, to set up a savings or checking account you will need an initial deposit, your Social Security number, and your ID or driver's license. You do not need to open an account at every bank (in fact, you shouldn't), but always have an account at the bank you order coins from and at the bank where you dump your searched coins. Remember to have a separate bank for ordering boxes and a separate bank for returning boxes! And do not forget to mark your searched rolls before returning them! If you decide to use a coin counter, make sure you understand where the bank will send the bagged coins later.

As always, dressing nicely, behaving well, and acting politely will get you a long way toward finding silver and having a positive banking experience. Be courteous, don't return short coin rolls, and open a savings or checking account if possible.

Saving and selling your coins

A s Bob's coin roll hunting collection grew, it became more and more difficult to keep track of the collection. He had so many different coin denominations and so many different varieties that storing the coins became a real challenge. When he accidentally mixed his 40 percent Kennedy half dollars with the 90 percent ones, the focus of his searches changed from coins to better organizational solutions.

Fortunately, Bob discovered the "Gold and Silver Collections" application. This iPhone application helped him to easily keep track of his coin roll hunting finds and collections. It even updated the current daily price of silver so he wouldn't have to! Opening the app each morning to check the current value of his collection became a welcoming start to the day. Never again would 90 percent silver coins be counted as 40 percent silver.

So, by now have you finally amassed a grand hoard of silver coins? Or did you just discover your first proof piece? In any case, you are probably wondering how best to store your coins.

Proper long-term storage can be essential to preserving the value of a coin; there are special cases,

2-by-2 inch cardboard holder

2-by2- inch plastic flip

cloths, and rooms designed particularly for the storage and display of high worth collectibles. However, the keepers that you find CRH require very little effort to maintain. The most important aspects of coin storage or display include security, safety, and organization.

Any coin that you have (or hoard of coins) should be saved in a secure environment to prevent theft. People store collectibles in all sorts of places. Shoeboxes in the closet and sock drawers in the dresser are fine for small collections. These locations offer perfect solutions for storing your CRH finds. As your collection grows in size and value over the years you may wish to purchase a small safe or lock box or deposit the more precious portion into a bank safe deposit box.

Unless you reside in a particularly unsound neighborhood, any of these storage means should suffice. The key to a secure environment seems to be keeping valuables hidden from view, in a location somewhat difficult to get to, and – perhaps most importantly – hidden from the minds of neighbors; if you do not want your collection stolen then do not talk publicly about your collection!

Although coins in a secure environment are protected from theft, they must also be kept in a safe environment and handled correctly to defend against accidental or natural damage. You will need to shield your coins from moisture, dry air, dust, and the scratches/damages that will result if they are dropped by mistake or handled incorrectly.

Plastic cases that seal air-tight around coins provide the best protection. These can be relatively expensive (25 to 75 cents each), but they are recommended for proof coins, higher-grade early date pieces, or any entity of greater value. Most of your loose silver pieces that retain only melt value (value derived solely from the precious metal content) definitely can be stored in rolls or bags. Some collectors choose to showcase pieces in special sets, folders, and binders

Coin collecting is a hobby for all ages.

with coin page inserts. There are also currency pages available for any notes that you have pulled aside, but these more expensive casings should be reserved for only your nicest pieces.

NOTE: Always hold valuable coins by the rim when moving them. Do not attempt to clean or polish your coins. Washing coins in any form (other than with a little water) will only eliminate any collectible value they may have had. Collectors buy unaltered and unwashed coins.

Inefficient organization will pose the final threat to your coin collection, especially as it grows in size and value. The organized CRH will create a spreadsheet or Word document to keep track of his or her collec-

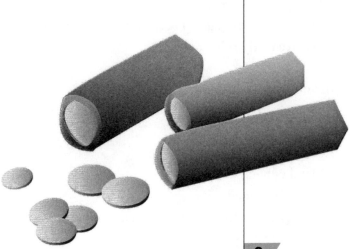

tion. Although expensive computer software exists with the function of organizing collections with fancy photographs and historical information, leave these and their lofty price tags to the advanced numismatist. A simple homemade spreadsheet containing the information listed below will work as well.

Also be sure to bear organization in mind when storing your coins. Decide which methods work best for you: rolls or coin tubes, bags, binder pages, cardboard flips, plas-

Q:

How should I keep track of the value of my coin roll hunting finds?

A:

Download the "Gold and Silver Collections" iPhone application.

tic cases, etc. Keep your coin denominations separate and always label your 40 percent and 90 percent silver Kennedy rolls.

In your spreadsheet include:

- Design of coin
- Denomination of coin
- Metal content
- Quantity owned
- Type of coin (precious metal value, proof piece, NIFC, error, special variety)
- Current value
- Total value of coin type
- Total collection value

Consider occasionally submitting your spreadsheet and several photographs of the collection to your insurance agency to guarantee extra protection.

Important Information about Selling Coins

After you have saved a few coins, you may decide that the time has come to start selling and taking some profit. Before you blindly begin selling your collection and risk losing potential profits, you should be aware of where your coin's value comes from and why people are willing to buy it.

The key characteristics of coins that shape their price are: condition, design, scarcity, date, mintmark, variety, metal content, historical influence, and market supply and demand. To value a coin you should take into account each of these factors separately and then together as a whole.

However, these values can change interdependently of each other. Therefore, to truly know the value of a coin you must not only break down the aspects of its worth, but also recognize which aspects hold proportionately greater influence on the particular coin's value. Because the prices of coins constantly change with the markets, the savvy collector will appreciate what characteristics form the value of a coin and understand how those traits will influence the price of the coin in the future. Here the "future value" of the coin actually affects its current value because of increased demand.

First, we will explore the supply and demand pricing component of a coin, which is formed by all of the other pricing characteristics of the coin and by the expected future value of the coin (and therefore its current demand and supply). This expectation of the future value of a coin shapes its demand, and consequently, to a great extent, its current price.

Fortunately, we won't worry about breaking down those characteristics described above to anticipate a future value here to determine demand. Because these values will already have largely been taken into account when we track the supply and demand of the coin in the current markets, they are not necessary.

Follow sales on eBay, at coin shows, and at local coin shops to develop a general "feel" for supply and demand in the coin marketplace. This method is actually far more accurate at determining the coins value because, obviously, it shows us the current sales values of coins. If we were interested in buying coins for investment, we would be better off deriving the future value of coins ourselves, identifying discrepancies between our value and the current market supply and demand, and taking advantage of those price differences ideally to make a greater profit in the future.

But, we aren't. So buy a copy of *U.S. Coin Digest*, published by Krause Publications, a necessity for any coin collector or coin roll hunter, and you are set.

The date, mintmark, variety, and design values of coins are easy to identify. Simply look at the coin, using a magnifying glass or loop if necessary, and find the date, mintmark (sometimes on the obverse sometimes on the reverse) and note the design. Open up your copy of the *U.S. Coin Digest* and find your specific variety.

NOTE: The price given in the *U.S. Coin Digest* represents the average price that dealers would generally list the coin to sell in their store. It is not meant to be a firm buy or sell price. Bullion coins that are valued for their precious metal content rather than any intrinsic numismatic value, fluctuate with the metals market. Prices will follow the price per troy ounce of gold and silver. A silver or gold melt calculator can help determine those prices.

The value of a coin to you, personally, can be very different from the value of a coin in the market. Although the silver dime you found may sell for $2.50 at melt value, technically you only paid 10 cents for it. If you didn't know what other people were paying for it, how much would you pay for it? Sometimes coins hold very little national historical importance but still signify great personal significance.

A proof coin from your birth year, for example, may be a piece you will not wish to sell. Just remember to make sure the dime and half dollar you were going to give to your grandparents at their next anniversary doesn't get lost in your bag of silver to be sold and melted. If the coin has more value to you or to a friend than it does to the general market, then don't sell it.

Two more items remain on our list: Condition and metal content. To better understand how commodity prices influence the melt value of a coin, please refer to the bullion section in the "Why to search and what to find" chapter of this book.

The important points to recall are:

1. Gold and silver prices change daily and greatly affect the values of coins that contain those metals.

2. Coins have different ratios of collectible value to precious metal value and these will affect the risk, relative to the commodity markets, of saving, buying, or selling those coins.

3. Higher commodity prices equate to greater market volume and fewer but more valuable finds while lower prices yield more coins available to find in circulation but at lesser values. The market supply and demand will always come to an equilibrium price and quantity, but coin roll hunters will always

receive coins for much lower prices.

To determine the standard melt value of a coin, multiply its metal content percentage times the weight of the entire coin (or simply take its content weight of the metal) and multiply that by the current price of the metal per ounce.

To practice, we will take a look at the metal content of a quarter, dime, and nickel. Imagine that you have just found a 1930 Standing Liberty quarter, a 1925 Buffalo nickel, and a 1964 Roosevelt dime.

The 1930 standing liberty quarter is composed of 90 percent silver. According to the *U.S. Coin Digest* book, this quarter contains .18084 ounces of pure silver. To find the silver melt value of this coin, multiply the silver component weight by the current silver spot price. So, if the spot price of silver is $30 per ounce, then the melt value of the quarter would be .18084 X $30 = $5.42!

The 1925 Buffalo nickel contains no silver. Therefore, the silver melt value of the nickel would be zero. This definitely does not mean that the coin is not worth anything. The nickel could be worth hundreds of dollars depending on the date and condition. However, there is no silver value to the coin.

Now, let's calculate the melt value of the 1964 Roosevelt dime. Dimes minted 1964 and earlier are made of 90 percent silver. According to the *U.S. Coin Digest* book, this coin contains .07234 ounces of pure silver.

To find the melt value, multiply the current spot price of silver by the silver content. With a silver spot price of $30 an ounce, the dime has a silver melt value of .07234 X $30 = $2.17. This 1964 Roosevelt dime is worth $2.17 at melt value! This means that at a minimum, no matter how common the date of this dime or how terrible the condition, the coin is always worth at least $2.17 for its silver content.

The "Gold and Silver Collections" iPhone application is the best tool available for keeping track of coin roll hunting finds and calculating melt values.

Silver Coin Chart:

Denomination	Years	Composition	Silver Weight	Appearance
Nickel	1942-1945	35%	0.05626 oz	Jefferson
Dime	Pre-1965	90%	0.07234 oz	Roosevelt & pre
Quarter	Pre-1965	90%	0.18084 oz	Washington & pre
Early Half Dollar	Pre-1965	90%	0.36169 oz	Kennedy & pre
Later Half Dollar	1965-1970	40%	0.14790 oz	Kennedy

The final key to coin evaluation can be the most difficult to deduce accurately. Coins are graded for condition according to the numismatic 1-70 grading scale, with 70 being the nicest condition and 1 being the poorest condition. Coins from 60-70 are considered to be in MS (mint state) or BU (brilliant uncirculated) condition. Coins from a never opened roll will all grade between 60 and 70. Toned (colored) or dirty coins can still score in this uncirculated range if the coin itself has not been scratched or worn. A coin in the 1-10 range will be extremely worn and will probably have only a partial (or no) readable date.

Most of the coins you will see in average circulated condition will grade between 20 and 50. Although the scale can be used very precisely with very valuable or high-grade coins, most refer to grades in their generality. For example, a "very fine" coin will describe a coin between 20 and 35.

Grade Categories:
• Poor 1
• Fair 2
• About Good (AG-3)
• Good (AG-4)
• Very Good (VG-8)
• Fine (F-12)
• Very Fine (VF-20) to Choice Very Fine (VF-30)
• Extremely Fine (EF-40) to Choice Extremely Fine (EF-45) or (XF-45)
• About Uncirculated (AU-50) to Choice About Uncirculated (AU-55) or (AU-58)
• Uncirculated (MS-60) to Choice Uncirculated (MS-65) to perfect (MS-70)

Proof coins will bear the designation PF instead of MS and only resemble coins between 60 and 70 on the scale.

Although you will see many coins selling with the detailed associations listed above, the general coin roll hunter only needs to refer to coins as:

Uncirculated: Great shape, nice coin, nice mint luster
About Uncirculated: Decent shape, perhaps some luster or shine
Average Circulated: Typical condition coin found in change (G-4 to XF-45)

AU-50

Indian cent

Lincoln cent

Buffalo nickel

Jefferson nickel

Mercury dime

Standing Liberty quarter

Washington quarter

Walking Liberty half dollar

Morgan dollar

Barber coins

VF-20

Indian cent

Lincoln cent

Buffalo nickel

Jefferson nickel

Mercury dime

Standing Liberty quarter

Washington quarter

Walking Liberty half dollar

Morgan dollar

Barber coins

G-4

Indian cent

Lincoln cent

Buffalo nickel

Jefferson nickel

Mercury dime

Standing Liberty quarter

Washington quarter

Walking Liberty half dollar

Morgan dollar   *Barber coins*

As you find more and more coins, you may decide to sell off portions of your collection. For example, coin roll hunters often will sell their silver bullion finds because of their higher values. Although most searchers will hold onto or collect their other finds, silver keepers usually are sold. To sell your silver coins you have several options: Sell them on eBay through auction, sell them to another collector or dealer at a coin show, or sell them to the local coin store or pawn shop. There are pluses and minuses to each transaction type.

Coin stores are great places to sell silver coins because they are almost always willing to buy them. Although coin stores need to make a profit and will generally offer lower prices than other buyers, they are a guaranteed source for a sale. If you have mainly bulk silver coins to sell, consider selling them there.

While coin shows offer more buyer variety, they

also require more effort on your part as the seller. Coin shows are monthly gatherings at convention centers or meeting areas where from several dozen to several hundred coin collectors and dealers gather to discuss numismatics and to buy, sell, and trade coins and currency.

Because there are so many buyers, you can ask around until you find an agreement you can settle with – the terms will almost always be more favorable than the often non-negotiable offer of your single local coin dealer.

Coin shows are also a great resource for meeting other coin collectors and learning more about numismatics, and are an exciting way to engage with the hobby and business of coin collecting. But, if you need to sell your coins immediately, you may not want to delay for the next available coin show, or risk transporting your valuables to the location for sale.

eBay and the rise of Internet popularity have made the online marketplace the largest arena for coin-related transactions. The large volume of global coin purchases and sales made online has transformed the numismatic marketplace.

The ease of the Internet has ensured that if you need to find a coin for your collection, it certainly can be found. Consequently, coin collecting has become easier and more efficient – and market prices have become more fluid and stable.

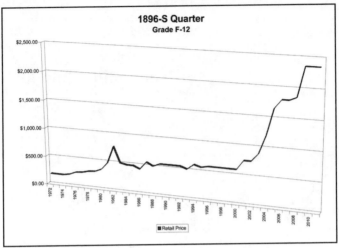

1896-S Quarter
Grade F-12

Value of an F-12 graded 1896-S quarter over time

If you have a very large quantity of coins, I highly recommend selling them online. By listing your bullion through auction you are guaranteed to receive the best market value at the time of sale. Although eBay charges a fee for the transaction, your extra profit will be greater than any loss. Furthermore, selling a large collection of silver coins together as one listing (called a lot) will significantly reduce the listing fees, as small as they were.

Although the method of coin sale will influence pricing, the appropriate time of sale relative to the current commodity price of silver plays the most important role. Deciding when to sell your coins can be a delicate decision that requires experience following market movements of silver and gold. Be sure to stay up to date on current commodity price fluctuations.

CHAPTER SEVEN

Advanced Strategies

Jake lived in the city. Like many other roll hunters he would stop by the bank each day to purchase rolls of half dollars.

Although Jake's finds were consistent, he became agitated one week after getting continually skunked during his searches. He would buy 10 or 20 rolls of half dollars a day from the branch, but the machine wrapped rolls would contain no silver. They didn't even give up any proof pieces!

Frustrated, Jake decided to skip the machine wrapped rolls at the branch one day. He would wait.

The next afternoon the bank offered him several shrink-wrapped rolls with red markings and two rolls with yellow markings wrapped by a different company. Jake decided to forgo the familiar red wrapped rolls and only purchase the coins in the yellow wrapping.

By selectively choosing which rolls to purchase, Jake reduced the rolls of coins he needed to search. Although the red rolls may have contained keepers, based on previous results from this branch, Jake decided that purchasing them wasn't worth the risk. In the long run, this strategy would help Jake find more silver coins per roll.

This chapter introduces several advanced coin roll hunting strategies. While these strategies are not terribly difficult to learn, they should only be attempted after mastering the basics. The coin roll hunter should be proficient at recognizing silver coins by the rim before applying these techniques. These methods are centered on the practice of identifying silver compositions of entire coin rolls.

When buying hand-wrapped rolls of coins from the bank, the silver composition is usually consistent. This technique helps to drastically reduce the quantity of coins unnecessarily searched. But be very careful. In order to make a conclusion about the composition of the remaining rolls you should go through at least two rolls first. Many coin roll hunters always search through every single roll, just in case. Coin roll hunters must decide whether to skip certain machine wrapped rolls depending on the number of rolls available and how much time he or she has to search.

Identifying Composition of a Coin Roll

You should have realized through your coin roll searches that some rolls of coins contain silver, and some do not. Although you may find one or two silver pieces in the last few rolls of a box of coins, this is usually unlikely. Because coins in boxes and rolls usually come from the same location or source, the composition of several rolls can help determine the silver composition of the other, accompanying rolls. Much time can be saved by selectively deciding which rolls to search.

There are four types of silver compositions in rolls of coins:

1. No silver
2. Occasional Silver
3. Steady Silver
4. Solid Silver

The first two types of silver compositions are the most common ones encountered coin roll hunting. 90 percent of the rolls you search will contain either no silver or the occasional silver coin. No silver composition rolls obviously, do not contain any silver. Occasional silver rolls typically contain one or two silver pieces every five to 10 rolls when searching rolls of half dollars or one or two silver pieces every 10 to 20 rolls when searching rolls of

Q:

Which denomination of coin rolls contains the most silver?

A:

Coin roll hunters will find the most silver by searching through half dollar coins.

Obverse mint mark
1916-1917

Reverse mint mark
1917-1947

Walking Liberty half dollar

dimes and quarters.

The silver composition in half dollar rolls, as you have probably already discovered, is usually higher than the silver composition of other coin rolls. This means that you will typically find more silver half dollar coins than silver dimes or quarters. This occurs because half dollars, unlike other denominations, were minted in silver until 1971. The U.S. ceased silver production in dimes and quarters much earlier. Additionally, there have been fewer half dollars produced for circulation than other coins. The U.S. stopped producing half dollars for general circulation in 2001, which means there are fewer modern half dollars at the bank than modern quarters and dimes. This means more silver!

Because half dollar coins are larger and contain

more silver, and because silver can be found more frequently in them than in rolls of other coins, coin roll hunters will generate most of their coin roll hunting profit through half dollar coins. However, because half dollar coins are less common at the bank, many coin roll hunters prefer to enjoy hunting dimes and quarters because of their availability.

Steady silver rolls continually produce silver when searched. These rolls are often older rolls that have not yet been searched or circulated in the past 10 years. Although some coin boxes will contain these types of rolls, most will not. Coin boxes are wrapped with coins coming from a very large source. Due to this, boxes of coins are usually more diluted than hand wrapped rolls; they usually contain mostly occasional silver rolls. However, sometimes a box will contain steady silver rolls – and when it does this means lots and lots of silver!

Usually, however, steady silver

Q:

When did we stop producing silver coins for general circulation?

A:

Dimes, quarters and half dollars were produced in 90 percent silver through 1964. We continued to mint half dollars in 40 percent silver through 1970.

rolls are hand-wrapped rolls recently deposited at the bank by an old coin collector. These collections are usually composed of one to 20 rolls of coins, usually half dollars. Although not every roll will contain silver, at least one-third, and probably at least half, will. Sometimes the rolls will contain two, three, four, or even five or more silver keepers! Chances are if you purchase a roll of coins at the bank, and it contains one or two silver pieces, the rest of the rolls there will contain some silver. This is where the strategy comes in.

When visiting a bank the teller may inform you that she has five rolls of half dollar coins in the vault, and two in her tray that she was hoping to give away to customers. You may decide to purchase the two rolls in her tray to check their silver composition. If neither of the rolls contains any silver, and the remaining rolls in the vault came from the same customer, then it is unlikely that any of the remaining rolls will contain silver either. Don't purchase them. However, if the original two rolls yield several silver pieces, then the rest of the rolls likely will too.

When buying hand wrapped rolls of coins from the bank, the silver composition is usually consistent. This technique helps to drastically reduce the quantity of coins unnecessarily searched. But be very careful. In order to make a conclusion about the composition of the remaining rolls you must search at least five rolls of coins. The first two or three rolls will often contain no silver – but the last may be filled with keepers. Additionally, this practice will not work if the person who deposited the coins separated the "old looking ones" from the newer ones. That last roll of 20 other clad rolls may very well be the only one with solid silver.

Yes, solid silver rolls. The big score. The grand finale. Every collector's dream come true.

Nothing is more exciting than discovering a solid roll of silver coins. This composition roll contains pure, solid silver. If one roll of half dollar coins contains only silver, then the rest will too. The searcher's largest find will come from a discovery of solid silver rolls. These coins have either been stored in the bank vault for a long time or they were recently dropped off at the bank by a customer unaware of their previous value.

Either way, solid rolls of silver coins are just as uncommon as they are valuable. A searcher is

Q:

Should I avoid searching through certain coin rolls?

A:

Enjoy the hunt and search every kind of coin roll.

lucky to find one or two of these in a year of searching. Finding more than three would be hitting the jackpot.

Despite the excitement and appeal of solid silver rolls, most of the silver you find will come from steady silver and occasional silver rolls. Although the finds may not be as large individually, the value that accumulates steadily from the other roll types will be more significant in your searches by far.

Currency

Coin roll hunters should also consider searching for older or antique currency.

Although at one time the government produced large-sized notes of circulation, you probably won't find any. Instead you will encounter many "old de-

Things to Save

- Older designs of currency (1970s-1990s) in nicer condition
- Star notes
- Error pieces
- Special serial number combinations
- Any note with a red or blue seal or note from the 1960's and earlier

How to Search

- Search currency by asking banks for "older" or "different" pieces
- The teller may be willing to scan through their currency for you
- Buying bundles of currency is costly and not effective
- Keep your eyes open for older pieces at retail stores too

sign" small-sized notes. You may find old designs or error pieces and may stumble upon a more valuable red or blue seal note from the 1950s or even a silver or gold certificate.

Since banks must submit older currency to the Federal Reserve to be destroyed, these notes have become increasingly scarcer and significant to the collector. There are also a variety of error pieces to be discovered. You may even find a star note bill (a note with a star next to the serial number). These notes are replacement pieces of currency for bills that became too damaged. Scarcer, early date star notes are extremely valuable – as are notes with strange serial number combinations such as all 1's or all 7's or any sequence of numbers.

CHAPTER EIGHT

Best Places to Search for Silver Coins

||||||||||||||||||||||||||||||||||||||||||||||||||||||||||||||||||||||||||||||||||||||||||||||||

W here are the best places to search for silver coins? Are some areas easier to search than others? This chapter examines the different types of coin roll hunting locations and the benefits of each. Let's take a look at the three coin roll hunting techniques (checking change, ordering boxes, and visiting banks,) and the location advantages of each.

Coin roll hunters should always check their pocket change, regardless of where it came from. The amount of silver and rare coins in general circulation is consistent across the United States. Sometimes even expert coin collectors mistakenly spend a silver dime or wheat back penny. In fact, most of the silver entering into circulation today comes from rolls of coins that were once saved by a coin collector or hoarder. Rare and valuable coins and currency can circulate at any time, any place, anywhere.

When searching through bank boxes of coins, the coin roll hunter may begin to notice some consistencies. Some bankrolls are hand wrapped while others are machine wrapped. Hand wrapped rolls come from individuals or tellers who have wrapped the coins.

These rolls may contain many silver coins or none at all.

Machine wrapped rolls of coins are wrapped and sealed by armored car companies. These firms do not search through the coins for silver. Because these machine wrapped coins come from a large variety of sources, silver coins are mixed together with clad coins in the rolls. Different boxes of coins may contain no keepers, one or two silver pieces, or ounces and ounces of silver, depending on when and where the coins were wrapped.

Generally, rolls that were wrapped years ago and have not been opened yet will contain more silver. Newer rolls are the most common to find, however. These newer bank boxes of coins can still contain a variety of silver. Many coin roll hunters order boxes of coins from banks to search each week.

Which boxes contain the most silver? Which banks deliver the best rolls of coins? Who should I order my boxes from?

Although coin roll hunters have argued that some armored car companies distribute rolls with more silver than others, not enough information is available to justify choosing one type of roll wrapping over another. Because machine sealed rolls contain mixed coins from an assortment of locations, coin roll hunters should not be picky when deciding where to order coin boxes. Always order coins from a bank where you have a checking or savings account.

The coin roll hunting possibilities are distinctive at urban and rural bank branches. Hand wrapped rolls will vary greatly from bank to bank. Often times, more rural areas will have older, hand wrapped rolls that have not yet been searched for silver. Older banks in rural areas

Q:

What are the three coin roll hunting techniques?

A:

Checking change, ordering boxes and visiting banks.

may have much silver stored away in the vault, waiting to be discovered. The key to searching banks in rural areas is to ask the tellers for hand wrapped rolls from the vault.

But remember, some coin rolls may have already been searched! Rolls with an X or other marking on them usually indicate a searched roll that was returned by another coin roll hunter. Additionally, some tellers may be aware of the value of their coins and search them as customers make deposits.

Coin roll hunters will have already searched most of the banks in more urban areas. However, city banks will also have many more customers making transactions. This means that the coins at these busier banks will change very frequently. Check banks frequently in urban areas so that you can buy any rare coins first, before anyone else does. Become friends with the tellers and they may even put special coins or currency aside for you. Another benefit of suburban and urban coin roll hunting is the proximity of banks. There will be more, closer bank branches typically within walking distance.

Keep in mind that valuable coins and currency can be found anywhere. Most coin roll hunters visit every single bank, regardless of location, size, or branch type. You never know what you might find. A roll of silver half dollars may have just been deposited at the busy bank branch that you have visited dozens of times. The bank in the middle of nowhere may be an untapped silver mine. Enjoy the weather, get some exercise, and walk through town to your local banks.

Coin roll hunters should budget time and gas to determine which banks they want to visit. Many coin roll hunters will check pocket change, order a box of coins from a local bank branch each week, and stop in at a few banks while on vacation or going into town. A trip dedicated entirely to coin roll hunting can be very exciting, but most will find integrating the searches into a current lifestyle more manageable. Will the coin roll hunting experience differ across the United States? Of course! Although the money in circulation is the same - towns, cities, and states will have different bank branches and different types of people. Areas with many coin roll hunters may be "dry" of silver for a while – but never permanently. Banks that had previously been over searched may eventually become unpopular spots, and in time they may again become the best places to visit.

You will steadily develop your own coin roll hunting strategy. Keep your eyes and ears open. If the tellers inform you that someone just stopped by their bank asking for half dollar coins, then maybe there is another coin roll hunter in town.

Coin roll hunting can be competitive – but there will always be more silver. The more coins that are found by coin roll hunters, the more coins that are sold to collectors, and the more coins that are again given away, passed along to relatives, or spent.

Coin roll hunters profit by finding free silver in circulation. Coins are bought at face value and sold for silver melt value (or much more!) Spread the love of coin roll hunting, learn techniques and share success stories with friends, and increase the amount of rare coins entering and exiting general circulation.

Because of the cyclical process of circulating silver coins, all areas of the United States will provide millions of ounces of silver each year. To optimize searching results, coin roll hunters should adapt their searches constantly to best suite the current environment. Recognize which banks and areas you enjoy visiting most and prepare to find hundreds to thousands of dollars of silver each year.

Q:

What are the benefits of checking rural banks?

A:

Rural banks may have older, hand wrapped coin rolls that have not been searched for silver.

Success and trial and error

III

It was a cloudy day in May, but I had just gotten out of school and I was in a good mood. On the bus ride home, I passed by several banks and wished that I were old enough to drive. I would be able to search through many coins if only I could get to the banks before they closed. I had been coin roll hunting for hours each week for months but had almost nothing to show for it. I didn't think I was doing anything wrong. I just needed to visit banks more frequently.

With the need to search for silver still close to my heart, I hurriedly consumed an afternoon snack and asked my mom if she could please, please drive me to our local bank. Graciously she consented and moments later we were out the door.

When I entered the bank I waited in line briefly before approaching the teller. A quick glance at her coin tray revealed no silver, but that was to be expected. I placed my wallet on the counter and greeted her kindly.

"Hello, I was wondering if you had any half dollar coins by any chance."

She looked puzzled. "Fifty-cent pieces you mean?"

My face brightened. "Yes, please," I said, "if you have any."

A roll of Morgan dollars

The teller opened her cash drawer and then quickly closed it. She paused for a moment then called out to the second teller.

"Do you still have those rolls of half dollars?" she asked.

How many rolls? I wondered. Eagerly I waited while the tellers dug out a dozen rolls of half dollar coins. The rolls were hand wrapped and looked rather worn. Although my heart was beating fast already, it jumped when the teller accidentally dropped one of the rolls onto the counter. The roll tore open and bright, shiny, silver Kennedy halves rolled out, their clink brightening the entire room. "We have $120 worth; would you like to buy them?"

My head pounded.

Quickly I handed her several twenties.

"I will take them all, please," I said. My hands shook with excitement and it took all I had to refrain from shouting out in victory. But I didn't hold the coins in my hand just yet.

Either by chance or because she heard the coins drop, the manager of the bank slyly appeared from a back door behind the counter. Her face was flushed with anger and another expression that resembled my own. I realized instantly that this manager knew the value of the coins.

The manager rushed over to the teller and calmly whispered. "Those coins are mine," she said. "I put them aside earlier so that I could buy them from the bank."

I began to protest and the manager's anger flourished. She shouted at me and demanded that I leave the bank branch immediately before I was reported.

Although I was an elementary school student at the time and

Q:

What is a silver half dollar worth? What would a full roll of silver half dollars be worth?

A:

At a silver spot price of $35 an ounce, a 90 percent silver half dollar is worth around $12. A full roll would sell for nearly $250.

therefore did not have the gumption to protest further, the teller, who also had been shouted at by the manager and was surprised by our poor treatment, supplied the argument that I was unable to. After much disagreement, the teller explained very clearly that because I was an account holder and customer of the bank, and because the manager had not yet purchased the coins, I had a right to them.

Quickly I paid the money, thanked the teller, and after a few shouts from the manager (who had somehow managed to snag a few coin rolls for herself) departed the bank. Flustered and a little bit scared, I hurried to the car and we drove off. It took me a full five minutes to finally open up the remaining coin rolls. Each one contained all 90 percent silver half dollars. Smiling, I closed my eyes and let my breath slow.

I realize now that the teller risked her position when she helped me. You never know what someone will do when they get their hands on some free silver if they recognize its value.

I have been to hundreds of banks coin roll hunting since that adventure and have yet to encounter an argument of such magnitude. All the same, I walked away with over $1,000 worth of silver that day – over 100 ounces! I have yet to find that much silver again at one bank.

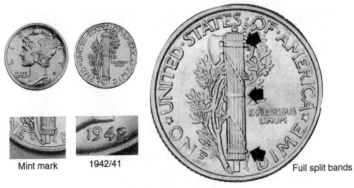

Mint mark 1942/41 Full split bands

1942/41Mercury dime

Persistence Really Does Pay Off

When playing a sport built upon chance, adhering to the most effective techniques will help you increase your odds and win the game. Trial and error has proven to be the best way to improve your searching behaviors. The more you search for coins, the better you will become at searching for them.

Soon you will develop a sense of which banks are best to frequent and which coins are best to search for. Similarly, the frequent coin roll hunter also will have more luck because he/she will ultimately journey through a much greater number of coins. The fact is that the more coins you search through the better you become at searching and the more chances you will have to encounter silver and rarities.

Coin roll hunters will not discover a hoard of silver overnight. But, with the correct form and continuous attempts, you will find silver – and lots of it.

COIN ROLL HUNTING CHEAT SHEET

SILVER GUIDE

The following coin denominations were minted in silver for the follow years:

Nickels 1942-1945
Dimes ....1964 and earlier
Quarters...................1964 and earlier
Half Dollars..............1970 and earlier

In addition to saving any special varieties, error coins, and proof pieces, keep an eye out for the following dates within each coin denomination:

CENTS

- Wheat cents and other designs minted 1959 and earlier
- Semi key and key date wheat cents include:

1909	1913-D	1921-S
1909-S	1913-S	1922
1909-S VDB	1914	1922-D
1910-S	1914-D	1924-D
1911-D	1914-S	1924-S
1911-S	1915	1931-S
1912	1915-D	1943 Steel
1912-D	1915-S	Varieties
1912-S	1916-D	
1913	1916-S	

NICKELS
- Nickels dated 1960 and earlier (including buffalo nickels)
- 1942 to 1945 35 percent silver war nickels

DIMES
- Dimes dated 1964 and earlier (Roosevelt, Mercury, Barber)

QUARTERS
- Quarters dated 1964 and earlier (Washington, Standing Liberty)

HALF DOLLARS
- Half dollars dated 1970 and earlier (40 percent silver)
- Half dollars dated 1964 and earlier (90 percent silver. Kennedy, Franklin, Liberty)

DOLLARS
- Any large dollar coins (Eisenhower, Morgan, Peace)
- Special varieties of smaller dollar coins (Susan B. Anthony, Sacagawea,Native American, Presidential)

CURRENCY
- Currency from the 1960s and earlier
- Red and Blue seal notes
- Silver and Gold certificates
- Large size notes and fractional currency

GOLD
- Any gold coins

COIN ROLL HUNTING RECORDS

Keep track of your coin roll hunting finds by bank. To keep track of your cumulative totals from all of your searches, please download the Gold and Silver Collections application for the iPhone from the iTunes app store.

Bank Branch: _____
Date: _____
Face Value Bought/Searched: _____
Denomination(s): _____
Coins Found: _____
Notes: _____

Bank Branch: _____
Date: _____
Face Value Bought/Searched: _____
Denomination(s): _____
Coins Found: _____
Notes: _____

Bank Branch: _____

Date: _____

Face Value Bought/Searched: _____

Denomination(s): _____

Coins Found: _____

Notes: _____

Bank Branch: _____

Date: _____

Face Value Bought/Searched: _____

Denomination(s): _____

Coins Found: _____

Notes: _____

Bank Branch: _____

Date: _____

Face Value Bought/Searched: _____

Denomination(s): _____

Coins Found: _____

Notes: _____

Bank Branch: _____

Date: _____

Face Value Bought/Searched: _____

Denomination(s): _____

Coins Found: _____

Notes: _____

Bank Branch: _____

Date: _____

Face Value Bought/Searched: _____

Denomination(s): _____

Coins Found: _____

Notes: _____

Bank Branch: _____

Date: _____

Face Value Bought/Searched: _____

Denomination(s): _____

Coins Found: _____

Notes: _____

Bank Branch: _____

Date: _____

Face Value Bought/Searched: _____

Denomination(s): _____

Coins Found: _____

Notes: _____

Bank Branch: _____

Date: _____

Face Value Bought/Searched: _____

Denomination(s): _____

Coins Found: _____

Notes: _____

Bank Branch: _____

Date: _____

Face Value Bought/Searched: _____

Denomination(s): _____

Coins Found: _____

Notes: _____

Bank Branch: _____

Date: _____

Face Value Bought/Searched: _____

Denomination(s): _____

Coins Found: _____

Notes: _____

Bank Branch: _____

Date: _____

Face Value Bought/Searched: _____

Denomination(s): _____

Coins Found: _____

Notes: _____

Bank Branch: _____

Date: _____

Face Value Bought/Searched: _____

Denomination(s): _____

Coins Found: _____

Notes: _____

Bank Branch: _____

Date: _____

Face Value Bought/Searched: _____

Denomination(s): _____

Coins Found: _____

Notes: _____

Bank Branch: _____

Date: _____

Face Value Bought/Searched: _____

Denomination(s): _____

Coins Found: _____

Notes: _____

Bank Branch: _____

Date: _____

Face Value Bought/Searched: _____

Denomination(s): _____

Coins Found: _____

Notes: _____

Bank Branch: _____

Date: _____

Face Value Bought/Searched: _____

Denomination(s): _____

Coins Found: _____

Notes: _____

Bank Branch: _____

Date: _____

Face Value Bought/Searched: _____

Denomination(s): _____

Coins Found: _____

Notes: _____

Bank Branch: _____

Date: _____

Face Value Bought/Searched: _____

Denomination(s): _____

Coins Found: _____

Notes: _____

Bank Branch: _____

Date: _____

Face Value Bought/Searched: _____

Denomination(s): _____

Coins Found: _____

Notes: _____

Bank Branch: _____

Date: _____

Face Value Bought/Searched: _____

Denomination(s): _____

Coins Found: _____

Notes: _____

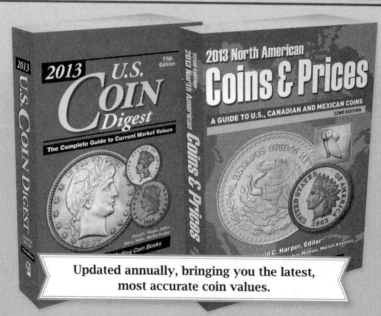

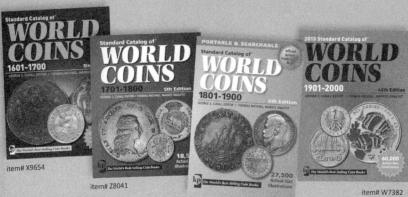